FAILURE MODES

FAILURE MODES

An Atlas of Psychological Systems

by J. A. Gucci

COPYRIGHT

Failure Modes: An Atlas of Psychological Systems
Copyright © 2026 by J. A. Gucci
All rights reserved.

This is a work of poetry. Any resemblance to actual persons or events is incidental.

Printed in the United States of America.

First edition.

ISBN: 978-1-972788-11-0

www.jagucci.com

"Composition precedes meaning."

5

PREFACE

These compositions do not describe psychological
states.
They construct them.

Each poem is governed by a physical system.
Meaning arises from behavior, not metaphor.

No interpretation is supplied.
The threshold is the reader.

CONTENTS

I. Signal Intrusion

Perceptual breaches · false inputs · contaminated awareness

II. Somatic Malfunction

Body as site · sensation without meaning · signal amplification

III. Affective Collapse

Flattening · inertia · tonal depletion

I. Signal Intrusion

*Perceptual breaches · false inputs ·
contaminated awareness*

Mandible Lock
297.1 — Delusional Disorder

Alight on a leafcutter—
seeping into stream.

Nervous networks—
sprawled
splayed
coiled on a leg
—fire.

Twitching up-stem—
jaws—
clenched on a green vein—

fruiting body.

Low Differential

300.02 — Generalized Anxiety Disorder

Slipstream—
flickering bulb—
boiler.

Wheezing radiator
spit—
dry air—

water hammer.

Marine Snow

300.6 — Depersonalization-Derealization Disorder

Ocean twilight—
strobing blue
electric,
green neon—
invisible.

Marine snow—
alight—
slimy silty skin.

Snap—
jagged needles—

empty
mouth.

Zenith Drop
347.00 — Narcolepsy

Zenith—
black slither—
flickering suns
scattered on asphalt.

Indigo sky—
lucent lunar valleys,

sharp shadows—
sheerless diamond ring.

Black face—
pigeon roost—

chirrups.

Sheltered Bay
300.12 — Selective Mutism

Spangled lamplight,
waves lapping
scree.

Warm breeze,
cool ocean gurgles—

white out—
black cove.

II. Somatic Malfunction

Body as site · sensation without meaning · signal amplification

No Shore
300.22 — Agoraphobia

Oily blue
glass lake—
shimmering seafloor.

Gloop—
salty coiled wave—

breathless,
buoyant—

pickled.

Salt Mirror
300.7 — Body Dysmorphic Disorder

Salty pink
brittle hexagons,

cacti on a hill,
blue—

long shadows
over slopes—
orange.

Rain.

Floating flamingos
alight on a cloud,
upside down—

moon—
red lagoon.

Spin Cycle
300.82 — Somatic Symptom Disorder

Steady—
whirring drum,
scum—
looping lathered
linen.

Blackout.

Locked legs
shuddering—
runaway drum—

scuffing.

Redolent Air
300.19 — Illness Anxiety Disorder

Sludge stench
shoe—

sniff,
scoff—

redolent—

sniff—
scoff.

III. Affective Collapse

Flattening · inertia · tonal depletion

Cold Start
296.23 — Major Depressive Disorder, Recurrent, Severe,
Without Psychotic Features

Ghost forest—

slumped over branch,
still—
clutching, twitching.

Twilight—

flickering eyelids—
frozen keel.

.

Fouling
300.4 — Persistent Depressive Disorder (Dysthymia)

Heartless—
hairy limbs,

jagged shells,
swamping—

glued to a hull.

Sinter

296.33 — Major Depressive Disorder, Recurrent, with Melancholic Features

Cold rain on lime—
drip
dribble…

Plink echos,
lithos—
a whistling blackbody.

Moonmilk—
sintered—
spearing soda straws
choked—

petrified.

IV. Identity Fracture

Multiplicity · absence · unstable self-reference

Dispersion
300.15 — Dissociative Identity Disorder

White light.

Cracked prism.

Red—
violet.

Electroreception

301.20 — Schizoid Personality Disorder

Knuckle walk—
glowing green—

toothless leather bill
sweating—
thirsty puggles.

Slit eyes—
ears,
electric heart beats
grind with gravel.

A tight embrace—
spurred.

Thigmonasty

301.83 — Avoidant Personality Disorder

Splayed green
poised under sun.

Waft of wind—

furled fingers—
a drooped stem—

leaking…

V. Relational Load & Distortion
Attachment failure · exploitation · dependence

File: Inflation

301.81 — Narcissistic Personality Disorder

Gushing inward stream—
spiked puffed pleats—

rigid sphere—
hollow,
gasping for air—

drained.

Dodder

301.50 — Dependent Personality Disorder

Dangling to duff—
reddish thin.

Thick,
grey braid—

hollow—
shriveling trunk.

Prickle

301.84 — Borderline Personality Disorder

Blue hour—
prodding prickle—
tugging.

Hooked by a barb—
bloody
undulating rib cage—
waning—

still.

VI. Stored Trauma & Release

Latency · discharge · environmental aftermath

Debris Flow
308.3 — Acute Stress Reaction

Cloudburst—
solid jagged peaks—
rocky steambed.

Squall—
snapped drunken trees—
splayed muddy toes
straddle the roadside—

creeping mountain—
smeared.

Permafrost

309.81 — Post-Traumatic Stress Disorder

Plucked—
scratched stone—
turquoise milk
flour in a lake.

Furry mammoths?
yellow wild flowers—

frozen
thaw.

Serotiny

312.34 — Intermittent Explosive Disorder

Shadowed—
emerald green—
fuzzy brittle logs—
petrichor.

Blazing canopy—
noxious air—

ash—
Jack pine.

VII. Cycles & Misalignment

Rhythmic failure · timing errors · ecological   mismatch

Tide Logic

300.3 — Obsessive-Compulsive Disorder

Ebb.
Flow.

Tender root—
deadfall.

Ebb.
Flow.

Cut notch—
sheer bluff.

Ebb.
Flow.

Sea arch—
teetering,
stacked.

Ebb—
slack water—
alarm flight.

Flow—
neap tide—
quivering aspen.

Super Bloom
296.40 — Bipolar II Disorder (Hypomanic Episode)

Autumn rain—
seeping.

Winter—
cracked seed.

Sun-baked—
wet
spring winds
wafting,

desert deluge—
California poppies.

COLOPHON

These poems were composed according to the
principles of Absolute Composition, where
structure precedes meaning.

Each poem is governed by a paradox triad—matter,
mind, being—and constructed through shifting
orbitals of compression.

Psychological states are rendered through physical
systems.